the WORD of PROMISE

From Jesus

We then, as workers together
with Him also plead with you not to
receive the grace of God in vain.

For He says:

*" In an acceptable time I have heard you,
And in the day of salvation I have helped you."*

Behold, now is the accepted time;
behold, *now is the day of salvation.*

2 CORINTHIANS 6:1–2

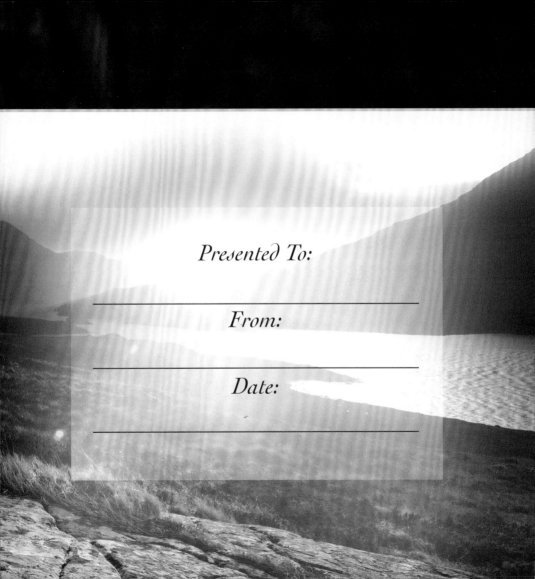

Presented To:

_____

From:

_____

Date:

_____

The Word of Promise From Jesus

Copyright © 2007 by Thomas Nelson, Inc.
Foreword © 2007 by Jim Caviezel

Published in Nashville, Tennessee, by Thomas Nelson, Inc.

Unless otherwise indicated, Scripture quotations are taken from *The Holy Bible*, New King James Version (NKJV) ©1979, 1980, 1982, 1992, Thomas Nelson, Inc.

Project Editor: Lisa Stilwell

Designed by Koechel Peterson Design, Minneapolis, Minnesota

Original music score composed and performed by Geoffrey Butterworth and Fred Legendre
Produced by 3:1 Studios, Smyrna, TN

ISBN 10: 1–4041–0496–8
ISBN 13: 978–1–4041–0496–9

Printed and bound in Belgium

www.thomasnelson.com

the
WORD of
PROMISE

From Jesus

Dramatic Passages from the Gospels

FOREWORD BY
JIM CAVIEZEL

Published by
THOMAS NELSON™
Since 1798

www.thomasnelson.com

Words of Promise

Jesus Presents the Beatitudes

The New Birth

Murder and Adultery Begin in the Heart

The Model Prayer

The Living God

Keep Asking, Keep Seeking

Jesus Forgives and Heals

Jesus Sends Out the Twelve Disciples

moving

inspired

timeless

The New Commandment

With God All Things Are Possible

Jesus Predicts His Death on the Cross

The Signs of the Times and the End of the Age

No One Knows the Day or the Hour

The Prayer in the Garden

The King on the Cross

Jesus Appears to His Disciples

The Great Commission

As you read through the Gospels, don't you sometimes wish you could stand on the banks of the Sea of Galilee and listen to the Master? Wouldn't you like to have been there when He turned water to wine, fed the five thousand, and gave Himself to us at the Last Supper? Imagine being on that fishing boat with the apostles and experiencing Jesus calming the storm or Peter walking on water. Think of the cries of joy that would have greeted Lazarus as he rose from the dead. And what must it have been like to hear the commanding voice and see the piercing eyes of the Son of God Himself?

We may not be able to go back in time, but we can bring the dramatic immediacy of that time into our own. This compelling presentation of moments from the life of Christ will stimulate your senses and pierce your heart. It will put you in the midst of history's most pivotal events.

When I had the opportunity to portray Jesus in the movie *The Passion of the Christ*, I was confronted by His reality: His humanity and awesome divinity. God took human form in a specific place and spoke words of truth to people like you and me. *He is still speaking.* My hope is that through this book and CD, you will hear the message of the Gospels anew and it will take root in your life. As you listen and turn the pages, let your imagination carry you back two millennia. Hear what God is saying to us today, right now. You will experience the Prince of Peace in an unexpected way and rediscover the true meaning of sacrifice, forgiveness, hope, and love. That is *my* word of promise to you.

Jim Caviezel

all eternity

Jesus Presents the Beatitudes

And seeing the multitudes, He went up on
a mountain, and when He was seated His
disciples came to Him. Then He opened
His mouth and taught them, saying:

"Blessed are the poor in spirit,
For theirs is the kingdom of heaven.
Blessed are those who mourn,
For they shall be comforted.
Blessed are the meek,
For they shall inherit the earth.
Blessed are those who hunger and thirst
for righteousness,
For they shall be filled.

Blessed are the merciful,
  For they shall obtain mercy.
Blessed are the pure in heart,
  For they shall see God.
Blessed are the peacemakers,
  For they shall be called sons of God.
Blessed are those who are persecuted
    for righteousness' sake,
  For theirs is the kingdom of heaven.

"BLESSED ARE YOU when they revile and
persecute you, and say all kinds of evil against you
falsely for My sake. Rejoice and be exceedingly glad,
for great is your reward in heaven, for so they
persecuted the prophets who were before you."

MATTHEW 5:1–12

The New Birth

There was a man of the Pharisees named Nicodemus, a ruler of the Jews. This man came to Jesus by night and said to Him, "Rabbi, we know that You are a teacher come from God; for no one can do these signs that You do unless God is with him."

Jesus answered and said to him, "Most assuredly, I say to you,

unless one is born again, he cannot see the kingdom of God."

Nicodemus said to Him, "How can a man be born when he is old? Can he enter a second time into his mother's womb and be born?"

Jesus answered, "Most assuredly, I say to you, unless one is born of water and the Spirit, he cannot enter the kingdom of God. That which is born of the flesh is flesh, and that which is born of the Spirit is spirit. Do not marvel that I said to you, 'You must be born again.' The wind blows where it wishes, and you hear the sound of it, but cannot tell where it comes from and where it goes. So is everyone who is born of the Spirit."

Nicodemus answered and said to Him,

"*How can these things be?*"

Jesus answered

and said to him, "Are you the teacher of Israel, and do not know these things? Most assuredly, I say to you, We speak what We know and testify what We have seen, and you do not receive Our witness. If I have told you earthly things and you do not believe, how will you believe if I tell you heavenly things? No one has ascended to heaven but He who came down from heaven, that is, the Son of Man who is in heaven. And as Moses lifted up the serpent in the wilderness, even so must the Son of Man be lifted up, that whoever believes in Him should not perish but have eternal life.

For God so loved the world that He gave His only begotten Son, that whoever believes in Him should not perish but have everlasting life.

For God did not send His Son into the world to condemn the world, but that the world through Him might be saved.

"He who believes in Him is not condemned; but he who does not believe is condemned already, because he has not believed in the name of the only begotten Son of God. And this is the condemnation, that the light has come into the world, and men loved darkness rather than light, because their deeds were evil. For everyone practicing evil hates the light and does not come to the light, lest his deeds should be exposed. But he who does the truth comes to the light, that his deeds may be clearly seen, that they have been done in God."

JOHN 3:1–21

MURDER AND ADULTERY
Begin in THE HEART

"You have heard that it was said to those of old, 'You shall not murder, and whoever murders will be in danger of the judgment.' But I say to you that whoever is angry with his brother without a cause shall be in danger of the judgment. And whoever says to his brother, 'Raca!' shall be in danger of the council. But whoever says, 'You fool!' shall be in danger of hell fire. Therefore if you bring your gift to the altar, and there remember that your brother has something against you, leave your gift there before the altar, and go your way.

First be reconciled to your brother,
and then come and offer your gift.

Agree with your adversary quickly, while you are on the way with him, lest your adversary deliver you to the judge, the judge hand you over to the officer, and you be thrown into prison. Assuredly, I say to you, you will by no means get out of there till you have paid the last penny.

"You have heard that it was said to those of old,

'You shall not commit adultery.' But I say to you that whoever looks at a woman to lust for her has already committed adultery with her in his heart.

If your right eye causes you to sin, pluck it out and cast it from you; for it is more profitable for you that one of your members perish, than for your whole body to be cast into hell. And if your right hand causes you to sin, cut it off and cast it from you; for it is more profitable for you that

You have heard...

one of your members perish, than for your whole body to be cast into hell.

"Furthermore it has been said, 'Whoever divorces his wife, let him give her a certificate of divorce.' But I say to you that whoever divorces his wife for any reason except sexual immorality causes her to commit adultery; and whoever marries a woman who is divorced commits adultery."

MATTHEW 5:21–32

THE MODEL PRAYER

"When you pray, go into your room, and when you have shut your door, pray to your Father who is in the secret place; and your Father who sees in secret will reward you openly. And when you pray, do not use vain repetitions as the heathen do. For they think that they will be heard for their many words. . . .

"For your Father knows the things you have need of before you ask Him.

In this manner, therefore, pray:

Our Father in heaven,

Hallowed be Your name.
Your kingdom come.
Your will be done
On earth as it is in heaven.
Give us this day our daily bread.
And forgive us our debts,
As we forgive our debtors.
And do not lead us into temptation,
But deliver us from the evil one.
For Yours is the kingdom and the power
and the glory forever. *Amen*

"For if you forgive men their trespasses, your heavenly Father will also forgive you. But if you do not forgive men their trespasses, neither will your Father forgive your trespasses.

"Moreover, when you fast, do not be like the hypocrites, with a sad countenance. For they disfigure their faces that they may appear to men to be fasting. Assuredly, I say to you, they have their reward.

"But you, when you fast, anoint your head and wash your face, so that you do not appear to men to be fasting, but to your Father who is in the secret place; and your Father who sees in secret will reward you openly."

MATTHEW 6:6–18

The living God

"Do not lay up for yourselves treasures on earth, where moth and rust destroy and where thieves break in and steal;

but lay up for yourselves treasures in heaven, where neither moth nor rust destroys and where thieves do not break in and steal. For where your treasure is, there your heart will be also.

"The lamp of the body is the eye. If therefore your eye is good, your whole body will be full of light. But if your eye is bad, your whole body will be full of darkness. If therefore the light that is in you is darkness, how great is that darkness!

"No one can serve two masters; for either he will hate the one and love the other, or else he will be loyal to the one and despise the other. You cannot serve God and mammon.

"Therefore I say to you,

do not worry about your life,

what you will eat or what you will drink; nor about your body, what you will put on. Is not life more than food and the body more than clothing? Look at the birds of the air, for they neither sow nor reap nor gather into barns; yet your heavenly Father feeds them. Are you not of more value than they? Which of you by worrying can add one cubit to his stature?

...do not worry

"So why do you worry about clothing?

Consider the lilies of the field,

how they grow: they neither toil nor spin; and yet I say to you that even Solomon in all his glory was not arrayed like one of these. Now if God so clothes the grass of the field, which today is, and tomorrow is thrown into the oven, will He not much more clothe you,

O you of little faith?

"Therefore do not worry, saying, 'What shall we eat?' or 'What shall we drink?' or 'What shall we wear?' For after all these things the Gentiles seek. For your heavenly Father knows that you need all these things.

But seek first the kingdom of God and His righteousness, and all these things shall be added to you.

Therefore do not worry about tomorrow, for tomorrow will worry about its own things. Sufficient for the day is its own trouble.

MATTHEW 6:19–34

...do not worry

KEEP *Asking,*
KEEP *Seeking*

"Ask, and it will be given to you; seek, and you will find; knock, and it will be opened to you. For everyone who asks receives, and he who seeks finds, and to him who knocks it will be opened. Or what man is there among you who, if his son asks for bread, will give him a stone? Or if he asks for a fish, will he give him a serpent? If you then, being evil, know how to give good gifts to your children, how much more will your Father who is in heaven give good things to those who ask Him! Therefore, whatever you want men to do to you, do also to them, for this is the Law and the Prophets.

"Enter by the narrow gate; for wide is the gate and broad is the way that leads to destruction, and there are many who go in by it.

Because narrow is the gate and difficult is the way which leads to life, and there are few who find it.

"Beware of false prophets, who come to you in sheep's clothing, but inwardly they are ravenous wolves. You will know them by their fruits. Do men gather grapes from thornbushes or figs from thistles? Even so, every good tree bears good fruit, but a bad tree bears bad fruit. A good tree cannot bear bad fruit, nor can a bad tree bear good fruit. Every tree that does not bear good fruit is cut down and thrown into the fire.

Therefore by their fruits you will know them."

MATTHEW 7:7–20

ask, seek, knock...

Jesus Forgives and Heals

So He got into a boat, crossed over, and came to His own city. Then behold, they brought to Him a paralytic lying on a bed. When Jesus saw their faith, He said to the paralytic,

"Son, be of good cheer; your sins are forgiven you."

And at once some of the scribes said within themselves, "This Man blasphemes!"

But Jesus, knowing their thoughts, said, "Why do you think evil in your hearts? For which is easier, to say, 'Your sins are forgiven you,' or to say, 'Arise and walk'? But that you may know that the Son of Man has power on earth to forgive sins"—then He said to the paralytic, "Arise, take up your bed, and go to your house." And he arose and departed to his house.

Now when the multitudes saw it, they marveled and glorified God, who had given such power to men.

As Jesus passed on from there, He saw a man named Matthew sitting at the tax office. And He said to him,

"Follow Me."
So he arose and followed Him.

Now it happened, as Jesus sat at the table in the house, that behold, many tax collectors and sinners came and sat down with Him and His disciples. And when the Pharisees saw it, they said to His disciples, "Why does your Teacher eat with tax collectors and sinners?"

When Jesus heard that, He said to them,

"Those who are well have no need of a physician, but those who are sick. But go and learn what this means: *'I desire mercy and not sacrifice.'* For I did not come to call the righteous, but sinners, to repentance."*

MATTHEW 9:1–13

Jesus Sends Out the Twelve Disciples

And when He had called His twelve disciples to Him, He gave them power over unclean spirits, to cast them out, and to heal all kinds of sickness and all kinds of disease. Now the names of the twelve apostles are these: first, Simon, who is called Peter, and Andrew his brother; James the son of Zebedee, and John his brother; Philip and Bartholomew; Thomas and Matthew the tax collector; James the son of Alphaeus, and Lebbaeus, whose surname was Thaddaeus; Simon the Cananite, and Judas Iscariot, who also betrayed Him.

These twelve Jesus sent out and commanded them, saying: "Do not go into the way of the Gentiles, and do not enter a city of the Samaritans. But go rather to the lost sheep of the house of Israel. And as you go, preach, saying,

'The kingdom of heaven is at hand.'

Heal the sick, cleanse the lepers, raise the dead, cast out demons. Freely you have received, freely give. Provide neither gold nor silver nor copper in your money belts, nor bag for your journey, nor two tunics, nor sandals, nor staffs; for a worker is worthy of his food.

"Now whatever city or town you enter, inquire who in it is worthy, and stay there till you go out. And when you go into a household, greet it. If the household is worthy, let

kingdom of heaven...

your peace come upon it. But if it is not worthy, let your peace return to you. And whoever will not receive you nor hear your words, when you depart from that house or city, shake off the dust from your feet. Assuredly, I say to you, it will be more tolerable for the land of Sodom and Gomorrah in the day of judgment than for that city!

"Behold, I send you out as sheep in the midst of wolves. Therefore be wise as serpents and harmless as doves."

MATTHEW 10:1–16

Jesus Teaches the Fear of God

"Whatever I tell you in the dark, speak in the light; and what you hear in the ear, preach on the housetops. And do not fear those who kill the body but cannot kill the soul. But rather fear Him who is able to destroy both soul and body in hell. Are not two sparrows sold for a copper coin? And not one of them falls to the ground apart from your Father's will. But the very hairs of your head are all numbered. Do not fear therefore; you are of more value than many sparrows.

"Therefore whoever confesses Me before men, him I will also confess before My Father who is in heaven. But whoever denies Me before men, him I will also deny before My Father who is in heaven."

Jesus Is *Lord* of the Sabbath

At that time Jesus went through the grainfields on the Sabbath. And His disciples were hungry, and began to pluck heads of grain and to eat. And when the Pharisees saw it, they said to Him, "Look, Your disciples are doing what is not lawful to do on the Sabbath!"

But He said to them, "Have you not read what David did when he was hungry, he and those who were with him: how he entered the house of God and ate the showbread which was not lawful for him to eat, nor for those who were with him, but only for the priests?

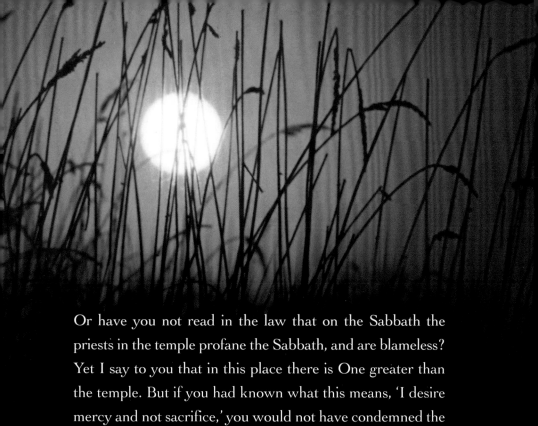

Or have you not read in the law that on the Sabbath the priests in the temple profane the Sabbath, and are blameless? Yet I say to you that in this place there is One greater than the temple. But if you had known what this means, 'I desire mercy and not sacrifice,' you would not have condemned the guiltless. For the Son of Man is Lord even of the Sabbath."

A House Divided Cannot Stand

Then one was brought to Him who was demon-possessed, blind and mute; and He healed him, so that the blind and mute man both spoke and saw. And all the multitudes were amazed and said, "Could this be the Son of David?"

Now when the Pharisees heard it they said, "This fellow does not cast out demons except by Beelzebub, the ruler of the demons."

But Jesus knew their thoughts, and said to them: "Every kingdom divided against itself is brought to desolation, and every city or house divided against itself will not stand. If Satan casts out Satan, he is divided against himself. How then will his kingdom stand? And if

I cast out demons by Beelzebub, by whom do your sons cast them out? Therefore they shall be your judges.

"But if I cast out demons by the Spirit of God, surely the kingdom of God has come upon you. Or how can one enter a strong man's house and plunder his goods, unless he first binds the strong man? And then he will plunder his house. He who is not with Me is against Me, and he who does not gather with Me scatters abroad.

"Therefore I say to you, every sin and blasphemy will be forgiven men, but the blasphemy against the Spirit will not be forgiven men. Anyone who speaks a word against the Son of Man, it will be forgiven him; but whoever speaks against the Holy Spirit, it will not be forgiven him, either in this age or in the age to come."

MATTHEW 12:22–32

the Son of David...

THE PARABLE
OF *the Sower*

On the same day Jesus went out of the house and sat by the sea. And great multitudes were gathered together to Him, so that He got into a boat and sat; and the whole multitude stood on the shore.

Then He spoke many things to them in parables, saying: "Behold, a sower went out to sow. And as he sowed, some seed fell by the wayside; and the birds came and devoured them. Some fell on stony places, where they did not have much earth; and they immediately sprang up because they had no depth of earth. But when the sun was up they were scorched, and because they had no root they withered away. And some fell among thorns, and the thorns sprang up and choked them. But others fell on good ground and yielded a crop: some a hundredfold, some sixty, some thirty. He who has ears to hear, let him hear!"

And the disciples came and said to Him, "Why do You speak to them in parables?" He answered and said to them, "Because it has been given to you to know the mysteries of the kingdom of heaven, but to them it has not been given. For whoever has, to him more will be given, and he will have abundance; but whoever does not have, even what he has will be taken away from him. Therefore I speak to them in parables, because seeing they do not see, and hearing they do not hear, nor do they understand. And in them the prophecy of Isaiah is fulfilled, which says:

'Hearing you will hear and shall not understand,
And seeing you will see and not perceive;
For the hearts of this people have grown dull.
Their ears are hard of hearing,
And their eyes they have closed,
Lest they should see with their eyes and hear
with their ears,
Lest they should understand with their hearts
and turn,
So that I should heal them.'

"But blessed are your eyes for they see, and your ears for they hear; for assuredly, I say to you that many prophets and righteous men desired to see what you see, and did not see it, and to hear what you hear, and did not hear it."

MATTHEW 13:1–17

THE PARABLE OF *the Sower*
EXPLAINED

"Therefore hear the parable of the sower: When anyone hears the word of the kingdom, and does not understand it, then the wicked one comes and snatches away what was sown in his heart. This is he who received seed by the wayside. But he who received the seed on stony places, this is he who hears the word and immediately receives it with joy; yet he has no root in himself, but endures only for a while. For when tribulation or persecution arises because of the word, immediately he stumbles. Now he who received seed among the thorns is he who hears the word, and the cares of this world and the deceitfulness of riches choke the word, and he becomes unfruitful. But he who received seed on the good ground is he who hears the word and understands it, who indeed bears fruit and produces: some a hundredfold, some sixty, some thirty."

MATTHEW 13:18–23

THE PARABLE OF THE
Wheat AND THE Tares

Another parable He put forth to them, saying: "The kingdom of heaven is like a man who sowed good seed in his field; but while men slept, his enemy came and sowed tares among the wheat and went his way. But when the grain had sprouted and produced a crop, then the tares also appeared. So the servants of the owner came and said to him, 'Sir, did you not sow good seed in your field?

How then does it have tares?' He said to them, 'An enemy has done this.' The servants said to him, 'Do you want us then to go and gather them up?' But he said, 'No, lest while you gather up the tares you also uproot the wheat with them. Let both grow together until the harvest, and at the time of harvest I will say to the reapers, 'First gather together the tares and bind them in bundles to burn them, but gather the wheat into my barn.'"

MATTHEW 13:24–30

Peter Confesses Jesus as the Christ

When Jesus came into the region of Caesarea Philippi, He asked His disciples, saying, "Who do men say that I, the Son of Man, am?"

So they said, "Some say John the Baptist, some Elijah, and others Jeremiah or one of the prophets."

He said to them, "But who do you say that I am?"

Simon Peter answered and said, "You are the Christ, the Son of the living God."

Jesus answered and said to him, "Blessed are you, Simon Bar-Jonah, for flesh and blood has not revealed this to you, but My Father who is in heaven. And I also say to you that you are Peter, and on this rock I will build My church, and the gates of Hades shall not prevail against it. And I will give you the keys of the kingdom of heaven, and whatever you bind on earth will be bound in heaven, and whatever you loose on earth will be loosed in heaven."

Then He commanded His disciples that they should tell no one that He was Jesus the Christ.

From that time Jesus began to show to His disciples that He must go to Jerusalem, and suffer many things from the elders and chief priests and scribes, and be killed, and be raised the third day.

Then Peter took Him aside and began to rebuke Him, saying, "Far be it from You, Lord; this shall not happen to You!"

But He turned and said to Peter, "Get behind Me, Satan! You are an offense to Me, for you are not mindful of the things of God, but the things of men."

MATTHEW 16:13–23

Take Up the Cross and Follow Him

Then Jesus said to His disciples,

"If anyone desires to come after Me, let him deny himself, and take up his cross, and follow Me. For whoever desires to save his life will lose it, but whoever loses his life for My sake will find it. For what profit is it to a man if he gains the whole world, and loses his own soul? Or what will a man give in exchange for his soul?

For the Son of Man will come

in the glory of His Father

with His angels, and then He will reward each according to his works.

Assuredly, I say to you, there are some standing here who shall not taste death till they see the Son of Man coming in

His kingdom."

MATTHEW 16:24–28

The *Way*, the *Truth*, and the *Life*

"Let not your heart be troubled; you believe in God, believe also in Me. In My Father's house are many mansions; if it were not so, I would have told you. I go to prepare a place for you. And if I go and prepare a place for you, I will come again and receive you to Myself; that where I am, there you may be also. And where I go you know, and the way you know."

Thomas said to Him, "Lord, we do not know where You are going, and how can we know the way?"

Jesus said to him,

"I am the way,

the truth, and the life.

No one comes to the Father

except through *Me."*

JOHN 14:1–6

The True Vine

"I am the true vine, and My Father
is the vinedresser.

Every branch in Me that does not bear fruit He takes
away; and every branch that bears fruit He prunes, that
it may bear more fruit. You are already clean because of
the word which I have spoken to you.

Abide in Me, and I in you.

As the branch cannot bear fruit of itself, unless it abides
in the vine, neither can you, unless you abide in Me.

Abide in Me...

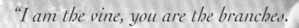
"I am the vine, you are the branches.

He who abides in Me, and I in him, bears much fruit;

for without Me you can do nothing.

If anyone does not abide in Me, he is cast out
as a branch and is withered; and they gather
them and throw them into the fire, and they are
burned. If you abide in Me, and My words abide in
you, you will ask what you desire, and it shall be done
for you. By this My Father is glorified, that you bear
much fruit; so you will be My disciples.

"As the Father loved Me, I also have loved you;
abide in My love. If you keep My commandments,
you will abide in My love, just as I have kept My
Father's commandments and abide in His love.

"These things I have spoken to you,

that My joy may remain in you,
and that your joy may be full.

This is My commandment, that you love one another as I have loved you. Greater love has no one than this, than to lay down one's life for his friends. You are My friends if you do whatever I command you. No longer do I call you servants, for a servant does not know what his master is doing; but I have called you friends, for all things that I heard from My Father I have made known to you.

You did not choose Me,
but I chose you and appointed you

that you should go and bear fruit, and that your fruit should remain, that whatever you ask the Father in My name He may give you. These things I command you, that you
love one another."

JOHN 15:1–17

THE *Work* OF THE HOLY *Spirit*

"These things I have spoken to you, that you should not be made to stumble. They will put you out of the synagogues; yes, the time is coming that whoever kills you will think that he offers God service. And these things they will do to you because they have not known the Father nor Me. But these things I have told you, that when the time comes, you may remember that I told you of them. . . .

"But now I go away to Him who sent Me, and none of you asks Me, 'Where are You going?' But because I have said these things to you, sorrow has filled your heart. Nevertheless I tell you the truth. It is to your advantage that I go away; for if I do not go away, the Helper will not come to you; but if I depart, I will send Him to you. And when He has come, He will convict the world of sin, and of righteousness, and of judgment: of sin, because they do not believe in Me; of righteousness, because I go to My Father and you see Me no more; of judgment, because the ruler of this world is judged.

"I still have many things to say to you, but you cannot bear them now. However, when He, the Spirit of truth, has come, He will guide you into all truth; for He will not speak on His own authority, but whatever He hears He will speak; and He will tell you things to come. He will glorify Me, for He will take of what is Mine and declare it to you. All things that the Father has are Mine. Therefore I said that He will take of Mine and declare it to you.

"A little while, and you will not see Me;
and again a little while, and you will
see Me, because I go to the Father."

JOHN 16:1–16

LIFE AND JUDGMENT
ARE THROUGH THE SON

When the people therefore saw that Jesus was not there, nor His disciples, they also got into boats and came to Capernaum, seeking Jesus. And when they found Him on the other side of the sea, they said to Him, "Rabbi, when did You come here?"

Jesus answered them and said, "Most assuredly, I say to you, you seek Me, not because you saw the signs, but because you ate of the loaves and were filled.

Do not labor for the food which perishes,
but for the food which endures to everlasting life,

which the Son of Man will give you, because God the Father has set His seal on Him."

JOHN 6:24–27

Jesus the *True* and *Good* Shepherd

"Most assuredly, I say to you, he who does not enter the sheepfold by the door, but climbs up some other way, the same is a thief and a robber. But he who enters by the door is the shepherd of the sheep. To him the doorkeeper opens, and the sheep hear his voice; and

he calls his own sheep by name

and leads them out. And when he brings out his own sheep,

he goes before them; and the sheep follow him, for they know his voice.

Yet they will by no means follow a stranger, but will flee from him, for they do not know the voice of strangers." Jesus used this illustration, but they did not understand the things which He spoke to them.

Then Jesus said

to them again, "Most assuredly, I say to you, I am the door of the sheep. All who ever came before Me are thieves and robbers, but the sheep did not hear them. I am the door.

If anyone enters by Me, he will be saved,

and will go in and out and find pasture. The thief does not come except to steal, and to kill, and to destroy. I have come that they may have life, and that they may have it more abundantly.

"I am the good shepherd.

The good shepherd gives His life for the sheep. But a hireling, he who is not the shepherd, one who does not own the sheep, sees the wolf coming and leaves the sheep and flees; and the wolf catches the sheep and scatters them.

The hireling flees because he is a hireling and does not care about the sheep. I am the good shepherd; and

I know My sheep,

and am known by My own.

As the Father knows Me, even so I know the Father; and I lay down My life for the sheep. And other sheep I have which are not of this fold; them also I must bring, and they will hear My voice; and there will be one flock and one shepherd.

"Therefore My Father loves Me, because I lay down My life that I may take it again. No one takes it from Me, but I lay it down of Myself. I have power to lay it down, and I have power to take it again. This command I have received from My Father."

JOHN 10:1–18

THE PARABLE OF
the Lost Sheep

"Take heed that you do not despise one of these little ones, for I say to you that in heaven their angels always see the face of My Father who is in heaven.

For the Son of Man has come to save that which was lost.

"What do you think? If a man has a hundred sheep, and one of them goes astray, does he not leave the ninety-nine and go to the mountains to seek the one that is straying? And if he should find it, assuredly, I say to you,

he rejoices more over that sheep than over the ninety-nine that did not go astray.

Even so it is not the will of your Father who is in heaven that one of these little ones should perish.

MATTHEW 18:10–14

Take heed...

DEALING WITH A SINNING BROTHER

"Moreover if your brother sins against you, go and tell him his fault between you and him alone. If he hears you, you have gained your brother. But if he will not hear, take with you one or two more, that 'by the mouth of two or three witnesses every word may be established.' And if he refuses to hear them, tell it to the church. But if he refuses even to hear the church, let him be to you like a heathen and a tax collector.

"Assuredly, I say to you, whatever you bind on earth will be bound in heaven, and whatever you loose on earth will be loosed in heaven.

"Again I say to you that if two of you agree on earth concerning anything that they ask, it will be done for them by My Father in heaven. For where two or three are gathered together in My name, I am there in the midst of them."

MATTHEW 18:15–20

Walk in the Light

Nevertheless even among the rulers many believed in Him, but because of the Pharisees they did not confess Him, lest they should be put out of the synagogue; for they loved the praise of men more than the praise of God.

Then Jesus cried out and said, "He who believes in Me, believes not in Me but in Him who sent Me. And he who sees Me sees Him who sent Me.

I have come as a light into the world,
that whoever believes in Me
should not abide in darkness.

And if anyone hears My words and does not believe, I do not judge him; for I did not come to judge the world but to save the world.

He who rejects Me, and does not receive My words, has that which judges him — the word that I have spoken will judge him in the last day. For I have not spoken on My own authority; but the Father who sent Me gave Me a command, what I should say and what I should speak. And I know that

His command is everlasting life.

Therefore, whatever I speak, just as the Father has told Me, so I speak."

JOHN 12:42–50

light into the world

THE NEW COMMANDMENT

So, when [Judas] had gone out, Jesus said, "Now the Son of Man is glorified, and God is glorified in Him. If God is glorified in Him, God will also glorify Him in Himself, and glorify Him immediately. Little children, I shall be with you a little while longer. You will seek Me; and as I said to the Jews,

'Where I am going, you cannot come,' so now I say to you. A new commandment I give to you, that you love one another; as I have loved you, that you also love one another. By this all will know that you are My disciples, if you have *love for one another."*

JOHN 13:31–35

WITH GOD *All Things* ARE POSSIBLE

Then Jesus said to His disciples, "Assuredly, I say to you that it is hard for a rich man to enter the kingdom of heaven. And again I say to you, it is easier for a camel to go through the eye of a needle than for a rich man to enter the kingdom of God."

When His disciples heard it, they were greatly astonished, saying, "Who then can be saved?" But Jesus looked at them and said to them,

"With men this is impossible,
but with God all things are possible."

Then Peter answered and said to Him, "See, we have left all and followed You. Therefore what shall we have?"

So Jesus said to them, "Assuredly I say to you, that in the regeneration,

when the Son of Man sits on the throne
of His glory, you who have followed Me
will also sit on twelve thrones,

judging the twelve tribes of Israel. And everyone who has left houses or brothers or sisters or father or mother or wife or children or lands, for My name's sake, shall receive a hundredfold, and inherit eternal life. But many who are first will be last, and the last first."

MATTHEW 19:23–30

Jesus Predicts His Death on the Cross

"Now My soul is troubled, and what shall I say? 'Father, save Me from this hour'?

But for this purpose I came to this hour. Father, glorify Your name."

Then a voice came from heaven, saying, "I have both glorified it and will glorify it again." Therefore the people who stood by and heard it said that it had thundered. Others said, "An angel has spoken to Him."

Jesus answered and said, "This voice did not come because of Me, but for your sake. Now is the judgment of this world; now the ruler of this world will be cast out. And I, if I am lifted up from the earth, will draw all peoples to Myself." This He said, signifying by what death He would die.

The people answered Him, "We have heard from the law that the Christ remains forever; and how can You say, 'The Son of Man must be lifted up'? Who is this Son of Man?"

Then Jesus said to them, "A little while longer the light is with you. Walk while you have the light, lest darkness overtake you; he who walks in darkness does not know where he is going.

While you have the light, believe in the light, that you may become sons of light."

These things Jesus spoke, and departed, and was hidden from them.

JOHN 12:27–36

The Signs of the Times and the End of the Age

Now as He sat on the Mount of Olives, the disciples came to Him privately, saying, "Tell us, when will these things be? And what will be the sign of Your coming, and of the end of the age?"

And Jesus answered and said to them: "Take heed that no one deceives you. For many will come in My name, saying, 'I am the Christ,' and will deceive many. And you will hear of wars and rumors of wars. See that you are not troubled; for all these things must come to pass, but the end is not yet.

For nation will rise against nation,
and kingdom against kingdom.

And there will be famines, pestilences, and earthquakes in various places. All these are the beginning of sorrows.

"Then they will deliver you up to tribulation and kill you, and you will be hated by all nations for My name's sake. And then many will be offended, will betray one another, and will hate one another. Then many false prophets will rise up and deceive many. And because lawlessness will abound, the love of many will grow cold. But he who endures to the end shall be saved. And this gospel of the kingdom will be preached in all the world as a witness to all the nations, and then the end will come.

"Therefore when you see the 'abomination of desolation,' spoken of by Daniel the prophet, standing in the holy place" (whoever reads, let him understand), "then let those who are in Judea flee to the mountains. Let him who is on the housetop not go down to take anything out of his house. And let him who is in the field not go back to get his clothes.

But woe to those who are pregnant and to those who are nursing babies in those days! And pray that your flight may not be in winter or on the Sabbath. For then there will be great tribulation, such as has not been since the beginning of the world until this time, no, nor ever shall be. And unless those days were shortened, no flesh would be saved; but for the elect's sake those days will be shortened.

"Then if anyone says to you, 'Look, here is the Christ!' or 'There!' do not believe it. For false christs and false prophets will rise and show great signs and wonders to deceive, if possible, even the elect. See, I have told you beforehand.

"Therefore if they say to you, 'Look, He is in the desert!' do not go out; or 'Look, He is in the inner rooms!' do not believe it. For as the lightning comes from the east and flashes to the west, so also will the coming of the Son of Man be. For wherever the carcass is, there the eagles will be gathered together.

power and glory...

"Immediately after the tribulation of those days the sun will be darkened, and the moon will not give its light; the stars will fall from heaven, and the powers of the heavens will be shaken. Then the sign of the Son of Man will appear in heaven, and then all the tribes of the earth will mourn, and

they will see the Son of Man coming on the clouds of heaven with power and great glory. And He will send His angels with a great sound of a trumpet, and they will gather together His elect from the four winds, from one end of heaven to the other."

MATTHEW 24:3–31

NO ONE KNOWS THE
Day OR THE *Hour*

"I was naked and you clothed Me; I was sick and you visited Me; I was in prison and you came to Me.'

"Then the righteous will answer Him, saying, 'Lord, when did we see You hungry and feed You, or thirsty and give You drink? When did we see You a stranger and take You in, or naked and clothe You? Or when did we see You sick, or in prison, and come to You?' And the King will answer and say to them, 'Assuredly, I say to you,

inasmuch as you did it to one of the least of these My brethren, you did it to Me.'

"Then He will also say to those on the left hand, 'Depart from Me, you cursed, into the everlasting fire prepared for the devil and his angels: for I was hungry and you gave Me no food; I was thirsty and you gave Me no drink; I was a stranger and you did not take Me in, naked and you did not clothe Me, sick and in prison and you did not visit Me.'

"Then they also will answer Him, saying, 'Lord, when did we see You hungry or thirsty or a stranger or naked or sick or in prison, and did not minister to You?'"

MATTHEW 25:36–44

The Prayer in the Garden

Then Jesus came with them to a place called Gethsemane, and said to the disciples, "Sit here while I go and pray over there." And He took with Him Peter and the two sons of Zebedee, and He began to be sorrowful and deeply distressed. Then He said to them, "My soul is exceedingly sorrowful, even to death.

Stay here and watch with Me."

Watch and pray...

He went a little farther and fell on His face, and prayed, saying,

"O My Father, if it is possible, let this cup pass from Me; nevertheless, not as I will, but as You will."

Then He came to the disciples and found them sleeping, and said to Peter, "What! Could you not watch with Me one hour? Watch and pray, lest you enter into temptation. The spirit indeed is willing, but the flesh is weak."

Again, a second time, He went away and prayed, saying, "O My Father, if this cup cannot pass away from Me unless I drink it, Your will be done." And He came and found them asleep again, for their eyes were heavy.

So He left them, went away again, and prayed the third time, saying the same words. Then He came to His disciples and said to them, "Are you still sleeping and resting?

Behold, the hour is at hand, and the Son of Man is being betrayed into the hands of sinners.

Rise, let us be going.

See, My betrayer is at hand."

MATTHEW 26:36–46

The King ON THE CROSS

Now as they led Him away, they laid hold of a certain man, Simon a Cyrenian, who was coming from the country, and on him they laid the cross that he might bear it after Jesus.

And a great multitude of the people followed Him, and women who also mourned and lamented Him. But Jesus, turning to them, said, "Daughters of Jerusalem, do not weep for Me, but weep for yourselves and for your children. For indeed the days are coming in which they will say, 'Blessed are the barren, wombs that never bore, and breasts which never nursed!' Then they will begin 'to say to the mountains, "Fall on us!" and to the hills, "Cover us!"' For if they do these things in the green wood, what will be done in the dry?"

There were also two others, criminals, led with Him to be put to death. And when they had come to the place called Calvary, there they crucified Him, and the criminals, one on the right hand and the other on the left. Then Jesus said,

"Father, forgive them, for they do not know what they do."

And they divided His garments and cast lots. And the people stood looking on. But even the rulers with them sneered, saying, "He saved others; let Him save Himself if He is the Christ, the chosen of God."

The soldiers also mocked Him, coming and offering Him sour wine, and saying, "If You are the King of the Jews, save Yourself."

Lord remember me...

And an inscription also was written over Him in letters of Greek, Latin, and Hebrew:

THIS IS THE KING OF THE JEWS.

Then one of the criminals who were hanged blasphemed Him, saying, "If You are the Christ, save Yourself and us."

But the other, answering, rebuked him, saying, "Do you not even fear God, seeing you are under the same condemnation? And we indeed justly, for we receive the due reward of our deeds; but this Man has done nothing wrong." Then he said to Jesus, "Lord, remember me when You come into Your kingdom."

And Jesus said to him,

"Assuredly, I say to you, today you will be with Me in Paradise."

Now it was about the sixth hour, and there was darkness over all the earth until the ninth hour. Then the sun was darkened, and the veil of the temple was torn in two. And when Jesus had cried out with a loud voice, He said,

"Father, 'into Your hands I commit My spirit.'"

Having said this, He breathed His last.

So when the centurion saw what had happened, he glorified God, saying, "Certainly this was a righteous Man!"

And the whole crowd who came together to that sight, seeing what had been done, beat their breasts and returned. But all His acquaintances, and the women who followed Him from Galilee, stood at a distance, watching these things.

LUKE 23:26–49

JESUS APPEARS TO
HIS *Disciples*

Now as they said these things, Jesus Himself stood in the midst of them, and said to them, "Peace to you." But they were terrified and frightened, and supposed they had seen a spirit. And He said to them, "Why are you troubled? And why do doubts arise in your hearts? Behold My hands and My feet, that it is I Myself. Handle Me and see, for a spirit does not have flesh and bones as you see I have."

When He had said this, He showed them His hands and His feet. But while they still did not believe for joy, and marveled, He said to them, "Have you any food here?" So they gave Him a piece of a broiled fish and some honeycomb. And He took it and ate in their presence.

Then He said to them,

"These are the words which I spoke to you while I was still with you, that all things must be fulfilled which were written in the Law of Moses and the Prophets and the Psalms concerning Me."

And He opened their understanding, that they might comprehend the Scriptures.

Then He said to them,

"Thus it is written, and thus it was necessary for the Christ to suffer and to rise from the dead the third day, and that repentance and remission of sins should be preached in His name to all nations, beginning at Jerusalem.

And you are witnesses of these things. Behold, I send the Promise of My Father upon you; but tarry in the city of Jerusalem until you are endued with power from on high."

And He led them out as far as Bethany, and He lifted up His hands and blessed them. Now it came to pass, while

He blessed them, that He was parted from them and carried up into heaven.

And they worshiped Him,
and returned to Jerusalem
with great joy, and were
continually in the temple
praising and blessing God.

Amen.

LUKE 24:36–53

The Great Commission

And Jesus came and spoke to them, saying,

"All authority has been given to Me in heaven and on earth. Go therefore and make disciples of all the nations, baptizing them in the name of the Father and of the Son and of the Holy Spirit,

teaching them to observe all things that I have commanded you; and lo,

*I am with you always,
even to the end of the age."*

Amen.

MATTHEW 28:18–20

Now Hear the Rest of the Story!
Listen as the entire New Testament comes to life!

the
WORD of
PROMISE:
NEW TESTAMENT AUDIO BIBLE

- Presented in Dramatic Audio Theater
- Starring Jim Caviezel as Jesus
- Also starring Marisa Tomei, Michael York, Richard Dreyfuss, Stacy Keach, Louis Gossett Jr., Kimberly Williams-Paisley and many other award-winning actors.
- Featuring an original music score by renowned Italian composer Stefano Mainetti
- A faithful rendering of the best-selling NKJV translation
- 20-CD Set, $49.99

www.TheWordofPromise.com

"If anyone has ears to hear, let him hear."
MARK 4:23

the WORD of PROMISE

NEW TESTAMENT
AUDIO BIBLE

PRESENTED IN DRAMATIC AUDIO THEATER

STARRING JIM CAVIEZEL AS JESUS

MARISA	MICHAEL	RICHARD	STACY	LOUIS	KIMBERLY
TOMEI	**YORK**	**DREYFUSS**	**KEACH**	**GOSSETT, JR.**	**WILLIAMS-PAISLEY**
AS MARY MAGDALENE	NARRATOR	AS MOSES	AS PAUL	AS JOHN	AS MARY, MOTHER OF JESUS

ALSO STARRING JOHN HEARD, LUKE PERRY, JOHN SCHNEIDER, ERNIE HUDSON,
LOU DIAMOND PHILLIPS, CHRIS McDONALD, MICHAEL W. SMITH
WITH TERENCE STAMP AS THE VOICE OF GOD, AND MANY OTHER AWARD WINNING ACTORS

NKJV

20
CD SET